THE TIGER

Ferocious Feline

Stéphanie Ledu-Frattini

Photos by Anup Shah/JACANA Agency

French series editor Valérie Tracqui

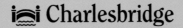 Charlesbridge

Published by Charlesbridge
85 Main Street
Watertown, MA 02472
(617) 926-0329
www.charlesbridge.com

Library of Congress Cataloging-in-Publication Data
Ledu-Frattini, Stéphanie.
  [Tigre. English]
  The tiger : ferocious feline / Stéphanie Ledu-Frattini ; photos
by Anup Shah/JACANA Agency ; [translated by Elizabeth Uhlig].
    p. cm.
Summary: Describes the physical characteristics, behavior, habitat,
life cycle, and endangered status of tigers. Includes bibliographical
references (p. 28).
  ISBN 1-57091-373-0 (softcover)
  1. Tigers—Juvenile literature. [1. Tigers. 2. Endangered species.]
I. Shah, Anup, ill. II. Title.
  QL737.C23 L4313 2003
  599.756—dc21   2002015718

Printed in China
(sc) 10 9 8 7 6 5 4 3 2 1

Photo Credits

All of the photos were taken by Anup Shah/JACANA Agency, with the exception of:
T. Davis/JACANA: pg. 6 (bottom); T. McHugh/JACANA: pg. 7 (left), 26 (top);
S. Cordier/JACANA: pg. 8–9, 10, 19, 26 (bottom); F. Savigny: pg. 11 (top);
E. Dragesco/JACANA: pg. 12 (bottom); AXEL/JACANA: pg. 15 (bottom left),
pg. 16–17, 17 (top right and bottom right), 18 (bottom), 20, 21 (top and bottom);
V. Thapar–P. Arnold/BIOS: pg. 24 (top); DANI-JESKE/BIOS: pg. 24 (bottom),
25 (top); G. Orlando/JACANA: pg. 25 (bottom); F. Polking/JACANA: p. 27 (top);
W. Pat/JACANA: pg. 27 (bottom); C. Haagner/JACANA: pg. 27 (middle).

CROUCHING IN THE SHADOWS

Summertime in India is stifling. The change of season from spring to summer turns the lush, green countryside into a yellow, dry savanna. By noontime temperatures can reach above 104 degrees Fahrenheit. All that is heard is the buzzing of insects. Exhausted by the heat, most animals rest.

Only the cleverest animals detect a tiger's presence. Tigers are camouflaged by their striped coats. Asia's largest predator, tigers spend their days sleeping in the dry grass, beneath huge fig trees. Every once in awhile, the great felines stir. During the day tigers spend their time cleaning themselves, drinking from nearby ponds, slipping into the water to cool off, or sleeping. Adult tigers are solitary animals, living alone in their territories except for females with cubs.

In the wild, tigers live only in Asia. They are found in all kinds of habitats from Siberia to Sumatra, including taigas, tropical forests, savannas, and swamps.

When tigers awaken, they stretch. This stretching stimulates tigers' circulation and helps sharpen their reflexes.

Tigers' territories always include bodies of water so that they may drink and stalk other animals that are drinking.

SUPER-PREDATOR

No two tigers share the same stripe pattern. From nose to tail, male tigers measure about nine feet long and weigh an average of 485 pounds. Females weigh about 300 pounds.

Tigers' whiskers tell them which way the wind is blowing and the width of the path in front of them. Their range of vision is very wide, and they see almost as well at night as they do during the day.

They hit the ground running, but after 650 feet, tigers get tired and stop. Better suited for leaping, tigers can jump 16 feet in a single bound.

A tiger's skeleton has more bones than a human skeleton. With their 600 powerful muscles, tigers are agile and lithe.

Tigers have sharp senses and their bodies are built for hunting. They are nocturnal hunters, beginning their hunt at twilight. Their night vision is six times better than a human's night vision. With their keen sense of smell, tigers can recognize a range of scents that go undetected by humans. Their ears turn with every sound they hear. Tigers even hear very fine ultrasounds, which are inaudible to us. Soft cushions on their paws muffle the sound of their steps. Despite all this tigers are only successful at catching prey one in 20 tries.

Adult tigers have 30 teeth with the upper canines measuring 3 inches long and the bottom ones measuring 1.5 inches long. Their sharp and retractable claws can grow as long as 4 inches.

PRIVATE PROPERTY

Every night, tigers inspect a part of their territory. If prey is plentiful, then tigers don't need much space. Covering about 20 miles, a male tiger's territory usually overlaps a female's territory. During their walks, tigers sniff the markings that they have left on the borders, which include bushes, tree trunks, and rocks. If a marking's odor has worn off, a tiger marks the place again with a mixture of urine and scent gland secretions. The musky smell can last for several weeks.

Tigers are clean animals and usually will not urinate in water where they drink or bathe.

Just like domestic cats, tigers sharpen their claws. Scratches on trees also serve as territory markers.

Sometimes male tigers will fight in order to conquer a territory.

Scents can inform tigers about the sex, age, and health of their fellow creatures. This tiger is leaving its scent on the tree.

Another way tigers mark their territory is by scratching the ground and defecating in the middle of their path. If a tiger detects the presence of another tiger in the area, it stops moving and holds still. If the intruder persists, the tiger uses intimidation tactics, such as roaring. More often than not, the unwanted visitor runs away. Tigers' roars can be heard for a radius of more than two miles.

HUNTING TACTICS

When animals leave their hiding places to find food and drink, it's hunting time. Tigers wait to ambush their prey. They crouch upwind, hidden near riverbanks in the tall grass, waiting and watching. Tigers wait for opportunities—like an older Sambar deer straying from its herd—to make their move.

With stomach low to the ground, tigers slink forward in great, smooth strides. Tigers will circle their prey in order to creep closer without being seen. From time to time, they stand still so as not to be seen. When they are on the hunt, tigers must sometimes wait a whole hour before they pounce on their prey.

Tigers approach their prey from behind. This allows tigers an advantage over animals heavier than they are and helps them avoid being hurt by an animal's antlers.

Tigers make surprise attacks, leaping at unsuspecting prey.

Plentiful in India, Sambar deer live in herds in forests and on steep terrains. These deer are prey for hungry tigers.

Tigers hunch their bodies as much as possible and leap at their prey, biting its hindquarters. They sink their teeth deeper and deeper into the animal's flesh. Tigers then bite their prey in the throat, causing the animal to suffocate and die. Sometimes with smaller prey, tigers bite the animal's neck, severing its spinal cord.

Tigers trap their prey and wait until the animal is exhausted before they finish it off.

Raspy Tongue

Like sandpaper, tigers' tongues have bristly little bumps. Tigers' tongues are rough enough that when they lick their prey they can make it bleed. With their tongues, tigers can clean all the meat off their prey's bones.

11

THE FEAST

Tigers don't always catch their prey. Most of the time, the prey is faster and gets away. Sometimes tigers go a whole week without eating. When tigers are lucky and catch something, they drag it into the bushes.

Once hidden, tigers devour their prey, starting with the hindquarters, their favorite part. They cut up the flesh with their sharp teeth and swallow more than 45 pounds of meat in a single meal. Tigers often drag their prey into the water to eat it. This way the smell of blood is not as strong, and scavengers will leave tigers to eat in peace.

Tigers need to eat about 15 pounds of meat each day. If they gorge themselves, tigers can go days without food. A grown deer is a perfect meal.

To discourage scavengers, tigers never leave the carcass, which will be their food for two or three nights. Tigers' favorite prey is deer and wild boar. They also eat monkeys, birds, fish, and even insects and frogs, if food is scarce.

Tigers attack scavengers like dholes (wild dogs), jackals, and vultures if they come near their food. But tigers will leave them any meat that is rotten.

When they are full, tigers clean themselves, removing any of the dead animal's blood from their fur.

MATING SEASON

Female tigers, or tigresses, can reproduce once they reach the age of three, and males can reproduce when they turn four. In November, the forest rings with howls of females in heat. Females stop hunting, and leave scent markings on their paths. They leave their territories to wander in the forest, in search of a partner.

A male tiger responds to a female with low growling sounds. The two tigers play with and tease each other. After this short courtship dance, they mate. In the course of one week, they mate about 20 times a day, and then sleep next to each other. Then the female grows aggressive toward the male.

Soon they each go back to their solitary lives and the female prepares to give birth. Males do not take part in raising their cubs.

Females let male tigers know they're ready to mate by scratching trees; this is also the same way they mark their territory.

After each coupling, the female tiger pushes the male away, growls at him, and tries to swat him. But after a few minutes, she goes back to him.

Sometimes two male tigers fight over a female.

During mating, the male tiger bites the female's neck in order to get her to keep still. When he is done, he lets her go and moves away.

GIVING BIRTH

For three months, female tigers spend much of their time hunting and eating a lot of prey as a way to build up their strength. When it's time to give birth, females walk around their territory in search of a hiding place that will shelter their cubs from the cold, rain, and predators. Ten days later, females give birth. A litter usually consists of two or three cubs. Cubs are about 16 inches long and weigh about two pounds each. They are born deaf and blind, and are completely dependent on their mother for survival. For the next three weeks, mothers will not leave their cubs, except to hunt. When mothers go off to hunt there is no one to watch their cubs, so many fall prey to predators.

At first cubs spend most of their time sleeping and nursing. Mothers take care of their cubs, licking them vigorously to help them eliminate waste from their bowels and bladders.

At the first sign of danger, mother tigers carry their cubs in their mouth to transport them to another shelter. It's painless: cubs just relax and let their bodies go limp.

All tigers have white patches behind their ears. Many people believe this makes it easier for mothers and cubs to find each other since the white patches are easy to see even in the tall grass.

SMART CUBS

Cubs grow quickly. They nurse until they are around six weeks old. At that time, they also begin to taste some of the food that their mother brings home. A mother's life is tiring because she has to find more and more food to satisfy her little ones' increasing appetites.

Mother tigers are very patient. They let their cubs bat at their ears and climb on them.

Mothers keep close guard over their cubs.

Mothers must make sure their cubs are safe. Before they go hunting, mothers bring their cubs to new hiding places. Cubs stay alone for many hours. Life is dangerous, so cubs don't risk going too far without their mother. They keep still and don't even play. When mothers return from hunting, cubs purr and rub against them.

Then cubs go off to chase each other and to scuffle. These activities help them develop speed and agility, which will be useful against predators.

Natural Selection

Female tigers can give birth to up to five cubs. Most of the time, females have two or three. The weakest cubs die at birth, and usually, only two cubs from each litter reach adulthood.

A young cub's first coat of fur doesn't offer protection from the cold. Cubs are easy prey for dholes and hyenas and would not survive if anything happened to their mothers.

HUNTING SCHOOL

When cubs are four months old, they can go with their mother for long strolls. Their mother shows them landmarks in their territory, such as watering holes and shelters, and teaches them to recognize prey. They are still too young to hunt, but they can watch their mother. Cubs must stay silent as their mother stalks prey. If they make noise and scare off prey, cubs will be scolded and swatted by their mother.

About three months later, their mother watches as her cubs try, as a group, to capture small prey. Their attempts to capture peacocks, partridges, squirrels, or hares may end in failure, but each try is good experience for cubs. Sometimes their mother brings back prey that she has disabled so cubs can practice their hunting techniques.

Young tigers often climb on branches and rocks to get a better look at their territory.

Bonds between cubs are very strong. They also constantly try to attract their mother's attention to gain her affection.

Cubs often imitate their mother's movements and practice stalking large prey.

GROWING UP

By the time tigers are 18 months old, they know how to spy on prey and ambush it. Now they have to learn how to pounce at the right moment and how to finish off prey. Often mother tigers start fights with small buffaloes or deer and then encourage one of the cubs to finish off the animals. Mothers watch, ready to intervene. Inexperienced tigers can get injured by a deer's antlers or can suffer a fatal kick from a hoof.

Little by little, family bonds dissolve. Young tigers' games become more brutal. Every day, each tiger goes off to explore the forest on its own. Sometimes, families come together a few hours later to share large prey.

At about two years old, tigers are adults. Mother tigers may already be expecting a new litter. It is time for each tiger to leave and find its own territory. After separating from their families, young female tigers settle in territories close to those where they were born. Males move farther away, in search of mates.

If they can avoid predators and poachers (people who illegally kill wild animals), then tigers can live 15 years.

Soon these young tigers will separate and find their own territories.

WILDLIFE IN DANGER

At the beginning of the twentieth century, there were more than 100,000 tigers. In 1960, only 2,500 were left. Humans have hunted tigers for their pelts and are responsible for this carnage. Today tigers are endangered animals. Many wildlife sanctuaries have been set up to ensure the tiger's survival.

A MAN-EATER?

In India, tigers present a danger to villagers. Every year, tigers kill about 200 people. Under normal circumstances, tigers avoid contact with humans. But in regions where tigers' natural sources of food are scarce because of deforestation, they have had to hunt and kill humans. Today, people are looking for solutions to this problem.

Today poachers are fined more than $8,500 for every tiger that they kill.

Organized Massacres

People have killed tigers, not just for their pelts but also out of cruelty. The maharajahs of India organized hunting parties during which hundreds of animals, such as elephants, bears, leopards, and tigers, were killed in a single day. The English, who colonized India during the nineteenth century, considered tiger-hunting a sport.

Indian police officers confiscate tiger pelts. Despite the intervention of the authorities, poachers kill wild animals every day.

Tigers won't attack people from the front. In order to walk through the forest safely, villagers wear masks on the backs of their heads.

OPERATION TIGER

Since 1969, tigers have been on the list of endangered species. It is illegal to hunt them or sell their fur. From 1972 to 1983, India and the World Wildlife Fund created 15 national parks that are considered "protective zones" and are off-limits to humans. In order to accomplish this, 12 villages were displaced. At first the people accepted Operation Tiger, but today, there are objections to it because tigers often attack herds of other animals.

Zoos try to safeguard remaining tiger species, but captive tigers can't be reintroduced to nature because they haven't learned to hunt.

AN UNCERTAIN FUTURE

Operation Tiger has allowed the tiger population to regenerate. Today, there are 5,000 tigers in India, 2,000 in Siberia, and 1,200 in Indochina. Human population growth and deforestation still pose a threat. Of the eight subspecies of tigers (Siberian, Bengal, Indochinese, South China, Sumatran, Caspian, Javan, and Bali), the Caspian, Javan, and Bali tigers are already extinct.

SIBERIAN TIGERS

Measuring approximately 11 feet long and weighing 705 pounds, Siberian tigers are the largest living felines. They live in Russia, China, and North Korea where temperatures can dip to –22 degrees Fahrenheit. During the winter, Siberian tigers' pelts thicken and become lighter in color.

FELINES

Tigers are the largest members of the feline family, which includes 35 other species. They share many similar traits with other species.

SERVALS

Servals' brown pelts have dark spots and stripes. They are small animals—about 32 inches long and weighing about 35 pounds. Servals are found in the tall underbrush of the African savanna. Solitary and generally nocturnal, servals creep up on their prey and pounce, often crushing their prey under their weight.

LEOPARDS

Also called panthers, leopards are fast felines that weigh between 83 and 128 pounds. They catch their prey and drag it up into a tree away from other predators so they can eat in peace. Leopards can give birth to both black and spotted cubs in the same litter. Once plentiful in Africa, the Middle East, and Asia, leopards are now endangered animals.

LYNX

Lynx vary in size and have small heads and enormous ears with tufts of fur at the tips. Well-suited to running, this excellent hunter prefers to live in wooded forests with dense undergrowth. Lynx can be found throughout the north in Europe, Canada, the United States, and Asia.

CHEETAHS

Cheetahs live on the African savanna. Of all the felines, cheetahs are the only ones whose claws are not retractable. These claws allow cheetahs to have better traction when running. Cheetahs are 48 to 56 inches long and can weigh up to 140 pounds. They can reach speeds of 70 miles per hour, making them the fastest mammals in the world.

For Further Reading on Tigers

DuTemple, Lesley A. *Tigers*. Minneapolis: Lerner Publications Company, 1996.

Harman, Amanda. *Tigers* (*Endangered!* series). Tarrytown, NY: Marshall Cavendish Corporation, 1996.

Levine, Stuart P. *Tigers* (*Nature's Predators* series). San Diego, CA: Kidhaven Press, 2002.

Schafer, Susan. *Tigers* (*Animals, Animals* series). Tarrytown, NY: Marshall Cavendish Corporation, 2001.

Use the Internet to Find Out More about Tigers

Cyber Tiger
—This fun site from The National Geographic Society allows kids to name their own cyber tiger and create a pen at the zoo for it by guessing what food and living space tigers need.

http://www.nationalgeographic.com/features/97/tigers/maina.html

5 Tigers: The Tiger Information Center
—The Tiger Information Center offers facts about and color photos of tigers. This site also includes information on the extinct species of tigers and has information for teachers.

http://www.5tigers.org/

Creature Feature: Tigers
—The National Geographic Society offers audio and video clips of tigers on this site. There are plenty of fun facts about tigers and even an electronic tiger postcard that you can send to a friend.

http://www.nationalgeographic.com/kids/creature_feature/0012/tigers.html

Index